Why Your Team Sucks

Learn To Inspire and Create a Winning Culture

GARETH NOBLE

Copyright © 2018 Gareth Noble

All rights reserved.

ISBN: 978-1-64370-020-5

DEDICATION

I dedicate this book to my wife. Also to my family and everyone who has helped shape my life's journey.

CONTENTS

Acknowledgments

1	Introduction	Pg. 9
2	The Vision	Pg. 12
3	The Leader	Pg. 18
4	Shut up – What Did You Say?	Pg. 27
5	Ubuntu	Pg. 33
6	Strategy	Pg. 37
7	Celebration	Pg. 43
8	Final Words	Pg. 46

ACKNOWLEDGMENTS

Why Your Team Sucks has been an extraordinary project. I am deeply grateful to everyone who contributed to making this dream a reality.

Special thanks to:
1. My Creator and King – through Him all things are possible.
2. The many leaders who helped me along the way.

1.
INTRODUCTION

I've learned more from my mistakes than anything else. I've learned so much from good strong leaders as well, but what changed my thinking and forced me to question my way of leading the most was looking back at the results of my leadership practices and the effect it had on people.

Most of what I learned about leadership is from hands-on, boots on the ground experience; in situations where you have to make a call. In my early years, when I had little knowledge of genuine leadership, I would lead thinking I knew what I was doing. When I messed up, and I did many times, there were consequences. You can't mess with people's lives. Being a leader means that you have a responsibility to whomever you lead. I'm not saying you're responsible for their decisions, but you're responsible for the information you give them because it influences their decision- making process.

This book is not about any particular research or an overload of information, but rather a guide to help and encourage your development as a leader through simple, intelligent and practical steps that get results. I use personal stories from my own life that were significant learning curves for me, which I know will be insightful and beneficial for you too. I have added some solid advice from other leaders that have inspired me and contributed to my journey concerning how I lead.

The development of a leader requires many things, but one factor stands out: **attitude**. I think if you have the right position you can accomplish anything and when I reflect on my life, I realize that it wasn't so much about talent and gifting that helped me become a decent leader but instead my attitude and how I responded to setbacks and challenges.

I desire to help you take your team from wherever they are to the next level. As a leader, it can be a daunting task if you're struggling and not sure what you are doing wrong. That's okay because I've been there and now, I'm here to help you figure it out. The secret to creating a winning team is all about learning vital skills and then applying them correctly. It takes energy and time, but when you do it intentionally, I guarantee you will see results.

The reason I decided to write this little book is to help leaders attain their full potential regardless of the stage they may be at in their leadership and team-building journey. It may be a sports team, a corporate group, a society, a church home cell or even a family – that doesn't matter – wherever you find yourself in the process, I will guide you by setting out a basic framework. If you're new to leadership and forming a team, this is an excellent place to start. For those more advanced, this book will serve as an encouragement and a reminder for what you should be doing.

This book will help you build a team that enjoys working together and whose members get excited about their organization. A group comprising of members who are in sync with one another, who buy into the vision of the organization is unstoppable.

2.
THE VISION

"Where there is no vision my people perish..."
King Solomon, Proverbs 29:18 KJV

I believe the biggest hindrance to an organization's success is a team that does not know where they are going, does not have someone to lead, has no clear mission and lacks the vital ingredient to becoming a formidable team – and that is vision.

They might be good at what they do, and their skill level may be high, but if there is no clear picture of what the results should look like, they merely exist. That team is operating in survival mode when they should be thriving. Mediocrity will be the norm – "the best of the worst and the worst of the best" as Neil Kennedy said. When things get tough, the team underperforms because there is no common purpose, members will work only for themselves, and there will be no reason for them to stay in the long run.

WHY YOUR TEAM SUCKS

A winning team builds upon a visionary leader who focuses on a common goal or dream. The vision of an organization should ignite passion and inspiration, and this is what will drive them through the tough times. An example of a man who has a tremendous vision for his life is Manny Pacquiao, one of the world's greatest boxers. Today, he ranks among some of the highest paid athletes in the world with an estimated net worth of $190 million according to Forbes magazine.

Born into poverty – Pacquiao is a fantastic example of someone who had a clear vision for his life and built a team around him to make it a reality. The Boxing Writers Association of America named this southpaw, "Fighter of the Decade."

Born in the year 1978, his story traces back to the southern part of the Philippines where he grew up abandoned by his father in extreme poverty. Manny's mother was left to take care of four children on her own. He dropped out of school at the age of 13 to sell bread and cigarettes to help provide for his family. Few would have imagined that this young boy would become one of the most exciting fighters and a world-boxing champion.

Against his mother's wishes, Manny decided to become a boxer. She wanted him to become a priest, but Manny told his mom they were too poor for that and he would make money by becoming a professional boxer. Soon, he stowed away aboard a ship set for Manila where he began training.

With no money to his name, Manny slept in the local boxing ring stained with the blood and sweat of other fighters. At 16, Manny was fighting professionally, which by law, was illegal, one had to be 18 years old. Because of his background, he was very skinny and undernourished. He hid metal in his shoes and pockets to reach the weigh-in goal.

However, Manny had a dream of becoming a pro athlete so he could take care of his family. His vision "to show the people of the Philippines that nothing is impossible when you have a dream." kept him focused and attracted his squad as well over time.

His sheer determination and vision for his life took him from a boy on the streets to a world champion, leader, and politician. Today, when Manny fights in a match, there is no traffic on the roads, even crime in the Philippines goes down to zero because everyone is glued to his or her television screens. When he isn't fighting, he is a businessman, singer, actor and a household name worldwide. This is the power of having a dream.

Believing the Dream

I agreed with James Kouzes and Barry Posner when they said that, "There's nothing more demoralizing than a leader who can't clearly articulate why we're doing what we're doing.", because when members of a team don't know what the dream looks like, they will always find an excuse as to why they can't get there. **People commit to what they believe in.** You must give your team something to believe in, a higher purpose. The vision outlines what your team will look like in the future. The vision must be more significant than an individual; it must stir you from the inside out. Great visionaries see the vision, great communicators reveal the vision, while exceptional leaders do both, they act by leading you to the summit.

WHY YOUR TEAM SUCKS

To better understand the correlation between vision and effective leadership, I would like to define some concepts that I will be talking about with regards to your team or organization. The mission or mission statement describes *what* a company wants to do. The mission outlines your objectives; it explains *how* you want to achieve results. The vision is a picture of what your team looks in the future. Your purpose is what fuels the team; it is the why, the reason behind everything you do. The mission statement supports the vision, and the purpose connects everything. The mission will build the company while the purpose will make the people.

When your team buys into the vision of your organization, their potential begins to shine through and take shape even amid hardship. When a team faces serious challenges, they will consider if it is worth their time and effort to overcome whatever the problem may be. When a leader has not clarified & communicated a vision worthy of sacrificing one's time, emotions, and other personal resources, the people in the group will eventually leave one after the other, depending on what their sell-out point is. In other words, without a clear vision, your team won't be sustainable.

As a leader, the first question you need to ask yourself is, "Do I have a clear vision for my company or team?" If you don't, you need to get one, and you need to communicate it clearly to your team, the sooner the better.

I've played on many sports teams in my lifetime and in the process I learned, though we put on the same jersey and wear the same color socks, it does not automatically make us a team. This happens at work, too. Just because you work in the same office and share the same coffee pot does not mean that you are part of a team.

Author Kristin Arnold explained this, "the vision and the mission is the glue that holds the team together." It is the leader's responsibility to cast that vision and make it clear so the team can run with it. The vision brings direction and unity to the team. When members of a group have a common purpose, it binds them together and gives them a deeper connection and understanding.

Once you have identified your vision, your mission and purpose become more evident, and you can then assess where the team is currently and make the necessary adjustments to get to where you want to go. The leader has to deliberately work on specific outcomes because he or she now has an understanding of what it takes to reach the target.

A great leader also must be able to identify critical activities and milestones that would help achieve the vision of his or her organization. Envisioning a preferred outcome and then stepping backward, repeatedly probing what must happen to enable each step has proven to be an efficient method in this regard.

Winning Culture

The team's vision is their destination, and without a map, they will never arrive there. When you understand your goal but have no plan, you won't find your way. Your vision is the destination, and your values are the map. Some of the values I talk about in this book include integrity, trust, empathy, courage, and commitment to name a few. When a leader demonstrates and drives these values, a high-performance culture emerges. Such teams have what I call a **winning culture**. Values shape the culture.

When a team begins to appropriate and embrace specific values, these values become part of who they are, and it becomes embedded in their DNA. Be patient; this quality will take some time to develop. The leader must intentionally teach, train and model these values daily. As a result; the team will begin to demonstrate and display these values, which is how we create culture.

3.
THE LEADER

"Leaders aren't born, they are made. And they are made just like anything else, through hard work. And that's the price we'll have to pay to achieve that goal or any goal."
-Vince Lombardi, American Football Coach

"The price of greatness is responsibility."
-Winston Churchill

A team rises or falls based on its leadership. We have seen that to be true for sports teams, big companies, and even countries. How one leads determines performance and sustainability. Previously, I explained how important vision is to an organization. With that said, a great leader is a visionary, one who sees the future.

Great leaders can inspire people to rise to any occasion. They have learned to be courageous and substantial for others. This type of leader knows how to rally his troops to get the job done whether or not they like him. When I think of a leader who exemplifies this, Winston Churchill comes to mind. Many people didn't like him; however, he was successful in uniting a country during difficult times and was tenacious in his approach as a leader.

I love what Dr. Miles Munroe says about having a spirit of leadership; he draws the analogy from the attitude of a lion. He goes on to say that the lion has a fearless mindset. He may not be the largest animal like the elephant, or the tallest animal like the giraffe or the fastest which is the cheetah. However, when he sees the elephant, he thinks "lunch." Even though the elephant is more powerful, it is afraid of the lion because of the lion's mindset. The lion believes he can eat the elephant, so he will attack the elephant. Our attitude is a product of our belief, and one cannot have an attitude beyond one's belief. The lion is the king because he believes in himself.

A Courageous Character

The dictionary definition of courage is "the quality of mind or spirit that enables a person to face difficulty, danger, pain, etc., without fear."

Just the other day, I heard a phrase that resonated with me: "Fear is what you feel; courage is what you do." To lead from the front, one must be brave. Therefore, a real leader is a risk taker who despite what he feels ventures into the unknown. All leaders need the spirit of conquest when it comes to their goals and aspirations.

Followers are attracted to these leaders because of this character trait, as having courage is something most people admire. Choosing to be brave and lead regardless of your feelings will automatically increase your team's confidence in you. They will begin to look up to you as someone with the strength and emotional intelligence to lead them to their destination.

Experiencing feelings of fear as a leader is normal, but you must learn how to manage your emotions. Being self-aware and in control of your feelings is an asset because it shows maturity and brings order to high-pressure environments where things may be out of control or chaotic. If you experience no fear at all, perhaps your vision is too small. Don't become comfortable in your leadership. Always move forward by asking yourself what the next level is.

For instance, when Alan Mulally arrived at Ford, he found that it was an exhausted organization which was losing $18 billion that year and had no intentions to address its fundamental issues.

To reorganize Ford's entire product line and convert the factories to mostly automatic operations, Mullaly borrowed $23.5 billion convincing the Ford family to pledge their stock and the famous Ford Blue Oval as collateral. His bold move paid off. Unlike its Detroit competitors, Ford avoided bankruptcy, regained market share and returned to profitability.

The Lifestyle of Learning

John F. Kennedy, a leader who inspired a whole nation to reach for the moon – despite the seemingly impossible nature of the goal at the time, declared in a speech in Dallas, one fateful day in 1963 saying,

WHY YOUR TEAM SUCKS

"Leadership and learning are indispensable to each other." Despite his assassination, the words of the US president acknowledged as one of history's greatest leaders, reminds us that leaders must always keep evolving.

Leaders are readers who soak up everything there is to know about successful leadership. If you want to have the competitive edge, you have to be hungry for growth as well as knowledge. When you stop reading and learning, you stop growing, which affects your leadership and this in turn, affects the growth of your team.

There was a notion a few years back that claimed leaders are born and not made. I disagree with that statement; I believe leaders raise leaders. The DNA of a great leader will eventually transfer to their protégés, provided that the students are open to correction and guidance. Becoming a leader is not a smooth process, it is an arduous one, but with the right mentor guiding you, anything and everything is achievable.

Strong leaders bring about change, which happens as a result of being trusted. A leader does not develop credibility overnight; it takes time. Great leaders that routinely line up their actions with their words build credibility and integrity, and that is something we don't often see in leaders today.

How do leaders in the 21st century build credibility, you may ask? They do this by consistently serving people and adding value to their team. If you want a formidable team, you need to be selfless at times. Perhaps, the reason your team sucks is your inadequacy as a leader, one who hides behind his or her title to bark orders at everyone. Stop projecting your character flaws onto your team. That is not leadership; that is mismanagement. People might obey you out of fear of losing their job, but they will never give you a 100 percent.

Great leaders influence others because of how they live their lives. Learn how to serve your team with your strengths, and they will follow you into any battle without an atom of doubt in their minds. A successful leader is one who has intentionally formed a committed group with members loyal to the cause. They become like their leader as they begin to emulate whom they see. We think no one is watching, but the truth is, there is always someone looking up to you.

Catch the Right Qualities

Certain qualities can be taught, and the rest can only be caught. When a leader works closely with their team and leads by example, team members will have the opportunity to absorb a lot more and do so at a quicker rate.

Exceptional leadership transforms a losing or mediocre team to a winning team. Around the year 1000 B.C. in the Ancient Near East, there lived a great leader named David who later became the leader of Israel. Before he became the king, he was an outcast who hid in caves eluding King Saul—the ruler at the time—who wanted David dead. The Bible reveals that over these many years he gathered up around 400 men described as losers, vagrants and misfits of all sorts. However, through the leadership of David, over a brief period, these men became formidable warriors who led armies and almost always came back victorious. A great leader will take their squad higher because, when you learn to become a better leader, your team automatically goes to another level.

Based on my life experience, I have put together 11 points you should avoid if you are aspiring to be a great leader;

1. Do NOT allow negative talk in your team.

Never entertain negative murmurs from your team, especially when it's about a fellow teammate. Gossip amongst your team members brings division in the camp and decreases morale. Let your team understand that you do not tolerate it. Contain the situation by dealing with any conflict as soon as possible. Teach your squad to take the initiative and responsibility by finding solutions to problems rather than exaggerating them.

2. Correct to PULL UP, not TEAR DOWN.

Leaders have their team members' best interests at heart. When they make a mistake, don't break them down. Be hard on the principle, soft on the person. Criticism must be constructive; otherwise it becomes destructive.

3. ALWAYS deal with issues on the RIGHT platform.

When an employee or team member causes harm to your organization, address the person accordingly. If someone messes up publicly, treat it openly, if someone messes up behind the scenes, correct that person privately. This demonstrates strong leadership and leaves no room for resentment to brew.

4. DON'T promote talent alone.

Do not place people in a position of leadership because of their talent or skill alone. Many make the mistake of putting talent before character. When looking for the right person, in regards to leadership, place more emphasis on attributes like attitude, faithfulness, reliability, and consistency. These traits can be taught and transferred to others.

5. DON'T make hasty decisions.

Always seek advice from your trusted inner circle of advisors. When you encounter forks in your journey, stop and take time out to think about your options and include your mentors as it will help to prevent you from making a wrong decision.

6. NEVER vent on social media.

In the heat of the moment, we say things that we shouldn't. Once you have posted something, it's out there for everyone to see. Refrain from sending that text, email or post that can be used against you. I have a rule when it comes to social media; if I'm skeptical about how my message will be received, I don't send it.

7. NEVER show discouragement.

If you or your team has hit a setback, don't show it. Your team will be looking up to you for direction. Have you ever seen a toddler trip and fall, then look up immediately to see if their mother is looking? They respond according to how their mom reacts. If she has a look of concern or shock, the child, in most instances, bursts into tears. An experienced mother makes light of the situation. She smiles and carries on like nothing happened and the toddler responds by getting up and continues to play. We can learn from this. See the situation as an opportunity to display your courage and tenacity by leading regardless of any failures.

8. DON'T underestimate your team.

You will be surprised as to what your team is capable of achieving. Don't be afraid to give them more responsibility. Challenge your team to reach excellence. Pressure can be positive; carbon morphs into a diamond under immense amounts of pressure. A team can transform when you set the right pressure on them. Have faith in your group and believe they can go to new heights. Having faith means acting on what you believe, and that is proof of faith in action. A leader that takes action gets results. Placing expectations on your team demonstrates your trust in them. Make sure you communicate your belief in their capabilities; this kind of affirmation produces inspiration. When you learn the art to inspire, your influence grows. In essence, this is what leadership is. Raise the bar, motivate your team and watch them fly.

9. DON'T give up.

We are all guilty of thinking of giving up; we have all felt like it, which is normal. Learn to push through to win the prize, run to win. Life is not a sprint; it is a marathon. When you learn the secret to motivating yourself, goals are soon achieved.

10. AVOID taking all the glory.

When you reach a milestone, receive an award or when you are recognized publicly for achievements; be sure to include and acknowledge your team.

11. ACKNOWLEDGE your limitations.

An excellent leader is one who takes responsibility when they mess up. Acknowledge your mistakes and don't be afraid to say, "I'm sorry." It is a reflection of strength and not of weakness.

The Higher Way

I want to encourage you today to become a stronger leader and pilot your team by both serving and adding value to them. Leaders are givers, not takers. A father will always give; he protects his family and takes care of them. A father takes responsibility; it is who he is. A leader has the same kind of heart. They lead even when it is not convenient for them.

A few years ago, I was a pastor at a church in a town just outside of Johannesburg. I recall spending time with the detectives at the local police station. Every week, for three years I would attend their internal meetings at the station. At the meeting, I would share a message, pray for them and teach on leadership principles. None of them were a member of my congregation; I did not get paid for this.

I willfully contributed to the community by taking responsibility for this team that needed support and encouragement. By adding value, consistently over a period, my influence with them grew. Soon, they were coming to me one by one for help with other personal challenges. Becoming a leader is not about having a title; it's about having the right mindset.

Many people think they are leading, but in fact, they are managing. A manager will tell you how to do it, and a leader will show you how to do it. People follow the manager because they have to; people follow a leader because they want to. The difference is in their approach and attitude. An exceptional leader understands that he must manage the work and lead the people; this is a better way of achieving results.

4.
SHUT UP – WHAT DID YOU SAY?

"When the trust account is high, communication is easy, instant and effective."
-Stephen R. Covey, *The Seven Habits of Highly Effective People*

Have you ever said something and the moment you did you knew that you shouldn't have, but it was too late? Perhaps you tried to take back what you'd said, but it only made things worse because it wasn't the right time to say it – I know I have. We all make mistakes, but some mistakes in life are avoidable. The bottom line is this: the things we say affect our lives and the lives of others.

I've done and said a lot of stupid things that I still regret today. I've said things that have landed me in trouble and caused me to lose money and friendships. I've said things that have hurt people that I wish I could take back. I can't, but I can learn not to repeat them.

That's why clear communication is vital to every aspect of our lives, especially within our teams. Without effective communication, units don't fire on all cylinders.

Unfortunately, we all live on the same planet, and sometimes it feels like we can't get away from each other even when we try. Learning how to work with all types of people to bring out the best in them is vital to your success as a leader. This world revolves around people—almost eight billion of us. The teams that learn to communicate clearly and effectively are the ones that get ahead, get what they want and thrive.

The Secret of a Great Communicator

A productive leader is required to know how to communicate with all members and elements of the organization, including employees, managers, customers and investors. He recognizes that each group may require a different communication style and leadership style and can adapt based on the audience. Practical communication skills are an essential aspect of any leader's portfolio of skills and experience.

People who communicate well can get things done because they pass a clear message across to their audience. This set of people connect with strangers effortlessly, thereby making transactions with them more comfortable and things like dialogue and ideas begin to flow.

Over the years, I've realized that many leaders with influence, position and power can say the stupidest things that cause the most harm. I've heard people who have tremendous responsibility say things that are way out of line and cause damage. These are people who earn big salaries and make huge decisions and run large organizations and sometimes, even countries.

I grew up in a dysfunctional home, in which communication was not our strong suit. For me, regular conversations were few and far between. Talks were more like shouting contests, especially between my twin brother and I. Growing up; we would fight so much that we were placed in separate classes during our years at school. Communication is a skill that I had to develop on my own to succeed in all areas of my life. How did I do it? I had to learn from others, and I also had to teach myself.

I learned a lot about communication during my years of playing team sport. Growing up in South Africa, from the age of six all the boys had to play rugby, and I loved it. I recall our halftime huddles when the captain encouraged us and spurred us on to victory. I always listened carefully and noticed more than just the instructions from him. I watched his body language; I listened to the tone of his voice. I also looked at the reactions of others towards this leader, this communicator. The captain was calm even under pressure. He would look each one of us in the eye and give instructions with authority which inspired us to offer our best for the team.

To this day, whenever I am around other people, I take the time to observe them. It's something you need to do if you want to become a master communicator. Learn from famous communicators on television, watch and pick up on things that make them stand out.

When the word *listen* is juggled, it spells the word *silent*. Effective communication involves exchanging information accurately. Exceptional communicators listen well. Teams that listen with the intention of understanding have the edge over teams that do not. Savvy communicators listen to the message; consider the emotions behind it, as well as the salient questions that surround it. You learn more by listening and not speaking.

Missing the Mark

Many people, including business leaders and managers, need constant practice to improve their skills, seeing as useful communication skills do not come naturally to most people. In addition to practicing, leaders should consider classes or training that will help them communicate effectively. There are many tools out there that one can use to identify whether their communication skills need improvement.

The most common reason why teams suck is *miscommunication*. The words you and I speak have a creative force within them. Words can be used to bring encouragement and hope and joy. On the other hand, they can bring destruction and pain. Think about the time someone close to you said something that hurt you; did it have a negative impact on you? Perhaps you felt sad or even angry.

Once spoken, words can never be retracted. How you use your words matter. There is a force within your words that can change things. Thankfully, I've learned to use my words to improve my future by encouraging others and myself. When I see something in my life that I don't like, I talk to it. For example, when I'm feeling lazy, and I begin to procrastinate, I will say out loud to myself "Come on Gareth, you've got this, go make it happen, you're a hard worker." Great leaders know how to use their words wisely, for the benefit of themselves and their team.

Speaking Words of Life

You must learn to talk to your future and give your words an assignment. Send them on a mission. The power of words is that they can go where you can't. Learn to send your words to those places you cannot reach. It will only be a matter of time before you get there.

Your words have a creative power behind them and can change the atmosphere. Sometimes a soft kind word can diffuse a tense situation. On the other hand, a robust authoritative word can bring an unfocused team back in line. It's essential that you learn to improve your communication with your team today.

One way to do that is by learning the recipe of success. The right ingredients will give you a fantastic dish, but, the right ingredients in the wrong proportions won't give you the same product. Wisdom knows how much of which component to use and when to use it. For example, there is a time to say something and times just to shut up.

Knowing when to say the right thing is critical. When I argue with my wife, and I become angry, I've learned it is better for me to keep quiet during the heat of the moment otherwise, I end up saying something I will regret. So I keep my mouth shut as much as possible until I have cooled down. Then I go back and speak calmly to her; this diffuses the situation.

On a corporate level, I've found that while facilitating team building programs, most were made up of knowledgeable and dynamic people that surprisingly lacked good communication skills. Make sure you take time to work on verbal communication dynamics with your team.

There are many good team building activities you can try in your workplace. When your squad practices and repeats these exercises, I assure you, their level of communication will improve.

5.
UBUNTU

"Whatever affects one directly, affects all indirectly. I can never be what I ought to be until you are what you ought to be. This is the interrelated structure of reality."
-Martin Luther King, Jr.

Ubuntu is a Nguni Bantu term meaning "*humanity*." It is often translated as "*I am because we are*" and also, "*humanity towards others.*" However, it is often used in a more philosophical sense to mean "*the belief in a universal bond of sharing that connects all humanity.*"

In this chapter, I would like to discuss the importance of collaboration. Working together as a team where everyone benefits will end up producing a winning culture. The leader, once again, must take ownership of this.

When a team member disconnects and becomes disengaged, the leader must be switched on to pick up on it early enough to remedy the problem. Your goal as a leader is to form a winning team. When a few members of a group are dissatisfied and disgruntled, it affects everyone else. When they are negative, it can quickly escalate. Soon, discord festers within the camp. A sharp leader should have a good relationship with each of their team members.

For more prominent corporations, the CEO or department head has to spend time with their inner circle—their team intentionally. Relationships are a significant key to productive collaboration.

Building the Winning Team

Building a healthy work environment where everyone thrives goes beyond the workplace. Excellent teams have the freedom to discuss whatever is on their minds with their leaders. The leader does not have to always agree with them but has to be compassionate enough to listen, understand and take some form of action to resolve the conflict.

I'm sure you've heard it said that *"people don't care how much you know until they know how much you care."* You can be highly educated and have a long title, but if you're not genuinely concerned about the wellbeing of your team, they will eventually pick up on it. I can quickly tell when a leader tries to get their people to serve their selfish dreams and personal agenda rather than the greater good.

I grew up in South Africa during the apartheid era. I was a teenager at the time when international pressure was put on the government for a free and fair democratic election to take place. I remember the looming fear of a racial civil war when Nelson Mandela was released from prison in 1990. The country was polarized and divided. A house divided from within cannot stand. However, a man who believed in freedom and equality rose to the occasion and through his leadership, our "*rainbow nation*" was birthed.

The outgoing president, F.W. de Klerk—who played a significant role behind closed doors—bought into the vision of a new and liberated country. Mandela's clear communication and vision for a united South Africa brought about a change that empowered the entire nation and propelled it onto the global stage.

Strength in Diversity

I believe there is strength in diversity. Many people are scared of uncharted waters. The fear of the unknown or the difference in others sometimes holds us back from embracing one another and working together for the common good. When we learn to receive each other regardless of race, language, religion and culture, we begin to open up to the possibilities of creating change.

I learned about real community when I worked for a nonprofit organization and lived in a mixed-race neighborhood called Alra Park in the East Rand area of South Africa. I was the only white person there – which seemed a little scary to me back then. However, in no time, I was eating in the houses of the families that made up that community as they learned to trust me. I might have looked a bit different on the outside, but I discovered that I was no different at all.

Beyond our skin color, we all had dreams, hopes for our families and fears for the future. In my three years living there, I formed friendships that still stand today. I am so grateful for the opportunity I had to live in this neighborhood.

Galileo once said, "*We cannot teach people anything, we can only help them discover it within themselves.*" In the same vein, a team will gain more strength by accepting the members with differences in opinion, culture, belief and educational background. If these people feel accepted, they will be motivated to support the goals and mission of whichever organization or community in which they find themselves.

Learn to harness each team member's strengths, embrace the diversity within your team and see how powerful it becomes.

6.
STRATEGY

"I am not afraid of an army of lions led by a sheep; I am afraid of an army of sheep led by a lion."
-Alexander the Great

Benjamin Franklin said, *"When you fail to plan, you plan to fail."* The reason why so many teams suck is: they haven't thought things through from beginning to end. The art of planning and coming up with clear operational action items is what separates the winners from the losers.

A team's mission statement is the *why*. Once you know your purpose and have a clear vision, the next step is the *how*. The *how*, is the strategy. I believe there is no perfect strategy, but a more efficient and effective way of accomplishing set goals.

It is essential to **involve your team when making decisions.** Learn to brainstorm with your team and get their input because sometimes it is often the quietest person in the room that has the best strategy. If you don't ask for input from introverted people, they probably won't give it. I have been a part of some teams where only the loudest or most confident ones at the table have a say. This usually happens when there is a hierarchy in place, and only select people get to speak their minds – The unfortunate result is so many fabulous ideas never get to see the light of day.

Ultimately, a leader makes the final decision. However, when each voice is heard, the decision-making process becomes more evident. Information is critical when it comes to making decisions. Data will determine a course of action, so it is super important to ask the right questions. Large corporations will pay hefty sums for the correct information which can make or break a company.

When people have the opportunity to share, and their thoughts and ideas are heard, it creates a sense of belonging and connection within the team. When we look for solutions from other people's perspectives, we begin to see the bigger picture.

Two things occur when you involve your team in planning your strategy:

1. You create a stronger team bond and sense of belonging.
2. Creativity and new ideas spring forth.

WHY YOUR TEAM SUCKS

Winning the War

Leadership and strategy go hand in hand; the ability to make quick decisions and take decisive action. It's the leader's responsibility to design the blueprint for the teams' success. However, some of the time, we are caught off guard by sudden changes that are out of our control, and that's life. The question is how do we adapt to these surprises? What do you do when your star quarterback gets injured early in a game? Alternatively, what course of action do you take when budgets are cut, and you were relying on a significant amount for a campaign?

I recently watched the 2018 American war drama, *12 Strong*. In response to 9/11, the elite U.S. Special Forces unit, *Operational Detachment Alpha 595*, was sent into Afghanistan. In the beginning, their mission was to rescue any pilots shot down during the war. However, the purpose quickly changed and became about convincing ethnic leaders in the area to join forces with them to better fight their common enemy: The Taliban and its Al-Qaeda allies.

I was impressed by the agility of thought displayed through the leadership of Captain Mitch Nelson. He had to make decisions quickly and change his unit's strategy in challenging conditions. They made use of limited resources and thought outside the box. Inspiring leaders are out on the front lines making the best of what they have, instead of complaining about what they don't have.

You may not have the resources of a multi-million-dollar company, but look at what you do have and use it to your fullest advantage. These soldiers took to riding on horseback to surprise the enemy. They managed to outmaneuver the opposition's heavy tanks because of the terrain. Nelson responded by improvising and gained the

Okay Coach

I've discovered that smart leaders hire people who are smarter than them. I advise organizations to hire consultants that specialize in particular areas in which they need a breakthrough. If you find your organization has "plateaued" or gone backward, do some research and choose a professional with proven results to help you get back on track. All it takes for significant steps forward is some expertise and experience.

As a leader, there were many times I didn't have the answer myself. That was a good thing because I knew it was an opportunity for me to learn something new. In those times, I would seek the guidance of my mentor. Having a mentor or coach can make a huge difference in your outcome. Find someone who is way ahead of you in the game and become his or her student.

Have you noticed that the number one tennis player in the world has a coach? Every gold medalist at the Olympics has a coach. You may have heard it said that, if you're the smartest person in the room, you're in the wrong place. This is because people who want to be the best are always looking for ways to improve and having this mindset will put you at an advantage.

When you connect with a mentor, you tap into all their years of experience and acceleration occurs. When you have someone like that in your life, someone that has gone further and achieved more, you can avoid so many mistakes and capitalize on their recipes for success. Learn from them and take their advice; it will be golden.

When you don't know what to do in a given situation; call them and ask them! It's important to find someone who is willing to invest in you. A real mentor will pass all of his knowledge and expertise on to the next generation. If you're restricted geographically or for some reason can't find the right person, read books and research online and learn remotely from the experts.

If you need advice on relationships, look for the family man who has stayed married for 50 years and has a healthy family. If you need financial information and your dad has been broke for the last 15 years, I don't think his advice will help you much. If you're looking to change your lifestyle with exercise and healthy eating habits, look for the personal trainer who looks like Arnold and not SpongeBob.

Hire people who can get you where you want to be. They know what is required to get to the top and they've already found a winning formula.

Imitate Excellence

Everyone loves to imitate success, but great leaders know when it is appropriate and when it isn't. I heard it said just the other day: ***Success leaves clues***. Imitate your mentor's virtuous behaviors, and eventually, you will reach their level.

We become like the people we spend time with. So, with whom are you hanging out? To whom are you listening? Success breeds success, get closer to those who are successful and share the right values.

Also, make sure to reassess your methodology. The way you do things is your modus operandi. Ask yourself if you and your team are effective. Are you getting the results you want to see? What needs to change? Seek the help and advice of people who can help you take your team to the next level.

7.
CELEBRATION

"Broadcasters calling a big game are often reminded to let the action breathe. A great moment of a televised game doesn't need any narration, which is why the announcers—the good ones, anyway—shut up at the celebration and let the pictures do the talking."
-Steve Rushin

Another reason why your team sucks could be because there is no team spirit and no camaraderie. Your team may have tasted some success, but it has left them without any real excitement. High-performance teams complement each other, and their leaders recognize and reward success. When we acknowledge the bravery or accomplishment of a team member, we begin to celebrate each other.

The most valuable resource you have is human capital. Your focus should be on developing and training them because when that happens, everything else will grow.

Many leaders focus on the building or the finances more than their people, and this is a mistake. The greatest asset you have is your team. Without them, there will be no real success outside of you. We should protect what is precious to us.

Team spirit is refreshing and uplifting, one can sense it within the camp. A sure way of creating momentum is when members of a team work hand in hand and have a win-win mentality. They understand the importance of their respective positions and work hard to achieve their personal and collective goals. This can be further illustrated by Coach John Wooden's words when he says, "Winning teams are characterized by unselfish team play." One of the greatest basketball coaches of all time adds, "I try to emphasize to my players that you must give to receive…This is something that holds true in basketball and life."

An Attitude of Gratitude

I've learned that gratitude is a leader's most powerful tool that is often underused. I once worked for a company where the leader was giving a pep talk. He told us, "I don't have to thank you for working here and doing your job." I was a little confused as what he was communicating was that he didn't need us and didn't value our contributions. As a boss, you don't have to thank everyone when they leave the office, but when they have worked hard on a project or put in extra hours to meet a deadline, make sure to recognize that and reward the effort.

I've learned that incentivizing the team with a bonus or maybe just thanking them publicly can create a buzz. Unfortunately, it's an area in which leaders often miss opportunities to connect with their team and where possible, reward them with new responsibilities and projects. Begin to create an atmosphere where people become excited to achieve something through recognizing their work.

Game, Set and Match

Think about when your favorite sport team scores in a tight game situation. What do you do? You jump up and down and scream or punch the air. That is because you have a connection with that team and are passionate about that team. Some go even further, on match day, they wear their team jersey and all the swag that goes with it. If enough people do that you can feel the electricity in the air. How can we translate that type of energy to the workplace?

Perhaps, as a leader, you need to spend more time with your team members and intentionally celebrate each one and thank them for their contributions. If you haven't done this, in a very long time, it could be the reason for your team's low morale.

All it takes is a little bit of initiative and planning, spending a small sum of money and celebrating your wins. You might be surprised what a difference it makes.

8.
FINAL WORDS

"The supreme quality for leadership is unquestionably integrity. Without it, no real success is possible, no matter whether it is on a section gang, a football field, in an army, or in an office."
-**Dwight D. Eisenhower**

The title of my book may be a bit harsh, but I wanted to make sure I caught your attention first. If you've gotten this far, it worked!

Over the years, I have had the privilege to go into prisons and share a message of hope with the inmates. I discovered that many of them proclaimed their innocence, that they were wrongfully accused. Regardless of the truth, I realized that the first step towards change is to acknowledge who you are. Sadly, many forfeit the opportunity for change. To advance your team, recognize their condition. Don't try to cover your team's flaws by inflating figures or exaggerating performance to make them appear better than what they are; this will delay everyone's growth. Some leaders will use these tactics to cloak their weak leadership and save face, but this will be short-lived. Rather own up and create a plan to remedy the situation.

Change is a powerful thing, and it can only take place when we practice what we learn in theory. Reading this book is good, but reading and then practicing what you have learned is so much better. Doers get somewhere. There are thousands of thinkers out there, but few doers.

Become a person of action. I want to implore you to take steps forward. Many people are afraid to take steps because of failure. Don't be scared to fail; failure is a good thing. It teaches you that you can try again and improve. Failure exposes what you shouldn't be doing, which will ultimately bring you closer to achieving your goals. Don't become someone that is afraid to make a decision.

Fear was a major stumbling block in my life. I was scared to try anything. You don't need anyone's permission to become the best version of yourself. Don't wait for their approval either. Just go ahead and do it, it's liberating.

Last Thoughts

I'm trying things today that I would never have imagined a few years ago. It's crazy. I had to work through my insecurities. I had to overcome my fears of what other people thought about me. I know what it feels like to always try to please people. That's too much pressure. According to some, I'm not qualified to write a book.

That's okay. I did it anyway.

For more information about speaking engagements and other inquiries, please visit: www.garethnoble.com

If you enjoyed the book, please leave a review for me on Amazon.com; I would appreciate it, as it will help me to publish more books like this in the future. Thank you for all your support!

Best always,
Gareth.

ABOUT THE AUTHOR

Born and raised in South Africa, Gareth Noble is an up and coming author, motivational speaker and leadership coach based in Dubai. With a background in sports technology, he has spent the last decade focusing on empowering athletes, corporate teams, youth organizations and nonprofits to resolve internal issues to bring out the best in their teams. He currently works as a teambuilding consultant for corporate organizations.

www.ingramcontent.com/pod-product-compliance
Lightning Source LLC
Chambersburg PA
CBHW021047180526
45163CB00005B/2316